The Mystery of Mars

Sally Ride and Tam O'Shaughnessy

CROWN PUBLISHERS, INC. ❦ NEW YORK

To our sisters—Bryn, Bear & Kim—

for their friendship, humor,

and love over the years.

Published by Crown Publishers, Inc., a Random House company,
201 East 50th Street, New York, New York 10022

CROWN and colophon are trademarks of Random House, Inc.

Printed in the United States of America

Library of Congress Cataloging-in-Publication Data
Ride, Sally
The mystery of Mars / Sally Ride & Tam O'Shaughnessy. —1st ed.
p.   cm.
[1. Mars (Planet).] I. O'Shaughnessy, Tam. II. Title.
QB641.R36   1999
523.43—dc21   98-52929

ISBN 0-517-70971-6 (trade) — ISBN 0-517-70972-4 (lib. bdg.)

November 1999
10 9 8 7 6 5 4 3 2

First Edition

Imagine a planet so far away that we see it as just a point of light in the night sky, yet so near that we dream of visiting it someday.

Gazing at Earth through the windows of the space shuttle, I looked down at the sparkling blue oceans, snowcapped mountains, and sprawling cities of the planet below. Above the horizon, I saw a familiar red point of light and wondered what it would be like to be in orbit around Mars. There, Earth would be just a pale blue speck of light, millions of miles away. The planet below me would be a rugged red world, with enormous volcanoes piercing through thin clouds, and sheer cliffs dropping off into huge canyons.

← Florida, through the window of the space shuttle.

↓ Earth and its moon from a distance of about 7 million miles. Our planet would look even smaller and fainter from Mars.

Imagine a planet so far away that we see it as just a point of light in the night sky, yet so near that we dream of visiting it someday.

Gazing at Earth through the windows of the space shuttle, I looked down at the sparkling blue oceans, snowcapped mountains, and sprawling cities of the planet below. Above the horizon, I saw a familiar red point of light and wondered what it would be like to be in orbit around Mars. There, Earth would be just a pale blue speck of light, millions of miles away. The planet below me would be a rugged red world, with enormous volcanoes piercing through thin clouds, and sheer cliffs dropping off into huge canyons.

4

← *Florida, through the window of the space shuttle.*

↓ *Earth and its moon from a distance of about 7 million miles. Our planet would look even smaller and fainter from Mars.*

It will be many years before astronauts visit Mars. But robot spacecraft have begun to explore that distant world. Through their eyes, we see a planet that is starkly beautiful, but cold, dry, and desolate. There is no water on its surface, no oxygen in its atmosphere, and no life in its soil. But we also see clues that ancient Mars may have been very different. Long, long ago, Mars may have been a warmer planet, with thick clouds, ice-covered lakes, and possibly even primitive microscopic life.

Over the years, we have learned a lot about this mysterious planet. But we still have many questions. If early Mars was different from the planet we see today, why did it change? Did primitive life evolve on Mars? If so, have any Martian microbes survived? This book describes what we now know about Mars and what we hope to learn about this intriguing planet in the future.

A mosaic of Mars pieced together from many photographs taken by the Viking *spacecraft.*

5

Ancient civilizations were as fascinated with the night sky as we are. When their scientists charted the heavens, they found that a few of the twinkling lights seemed to wander across the sky against the background of stars. These were called planets, which is from the Greek word for "wanderers." One of the brightest had a reddish color and was later named Mars, after the Roman god of war.

Many hundreds of years later, scientists painstakingly plotted the path of Mars across the sky and learned that this planet, like Earth, orbits the sun. Their observations showed that Mars travels around the sun in about two years and that Mars is Earth's neighbor in the solar system. Earth is the third planet from the sun. Mars is the fourth.

With the invention of the telescope in the 1600s, astronomers had a much better view of Mars. Instead of seeing just a twinkling reddish light, scientists got a blurry view of a large, round world—maybe a world like Earth.

They measured the size of the image in their telescopes and discovered that Mars was a smaller planet than Earth. The distance across Mars at the equator is about half the distance across Earth.

As telescopes improved, the blurry disk came a bit more into focus. The north and south poles of Mars, like those of Earth, appeared to be covered with icecaps. And

some parts of the Martian surface were definitely darker than others. As astronomers watched these markings through their telescopes, they noticed that this planet, like Earth, was rotating—spinning like a top. They timed the rotation and found that Mars spins around once every 24 hours and 37 minutes, which means that a day on Mars is just a little longer than a day on Earth.

The size and shape of the fuzzy, dark areas changed with the Martian seasons. Some astronomers thought that these areas looked vaguely green. Could they be vegetation? If so, could there also be other forms of life—maybe even civilizations—on this faraway world?

Mars' orbit is approximately one and a half times the size of Earth's. (For clarity, the inner planets, Mercury and Venus, are not shown. The sizes of the sun and planets are not to scale.)

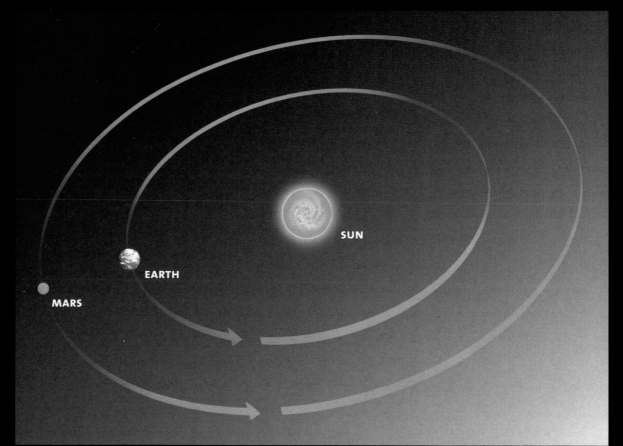

MARS

EARTH

SUN

A DAY ON MARS

On Mars, the sun rises in the morning, climbs in the sky, and sets in the evening, just as it does on Earth. This is because Mars, like Earth, rotates about its axis while it is traveling around the sun. To a person standing on the rotating planet, it looks as if the sun is moving across the sky.

A day on Earth is 24 hours long because it takes our planet 24 hours to make one complete rotation. Mars rotates at about the same rate as Earth. It takes Mars 24 hours and 37 minutes to spin around once. A day on Mars, called a sol (the Latin word for "sun"), is 37 minutes longer than a day on Earth.

On some other planets, a "day" is very different. A day on Venus is very long—244 Earth days! This is because Venus rotates very slowly, only once every 244 days. A day on Jupiter is very short—only 10 hours long—because Jupiter rotates very quickly.

AS MARS SPINS, A PARTICULAR PLACE ON ITS SURFACE MOVES FROM DARKNESS TO DAWN, THEN TO DAYLIGHT.

A YEAR ON MARS

A year on Earth—365 days—is the time it takes our planet to travel around the sun. Mars is farther from the sun, so it takes longer to go around. A year on Mars is 687 Earth days, nearly two Earth years.

On Earth, each year has four seasons: spring, summer, fall, and winter. We have seasons because Earth's rotation axis is tilted.

When Earth is at (A) in its orbit around the sun, the sunlight shines more directly on the northern half of the planet. A city north of the equator is in daylight for more than 12 hours a day. It is summer in the Northern Hemisphere and winter in the Southern Hemisphere.

Six months later, the Earth is halfway around in its orbit (B). Now the sun shines more directly on the southern half of the planet. At this time of the year, it is summer in the Southern Hemisphere and winter in the Northern Hemisphere.

Earth's axis is tilted about 23.5 degrees. Mars is also tilted, about 25 degrees, nearly the same as Earth. So Mars also has a winter, spring, summer, and fall. The biggest difference is that since a Martian year is twice as long as an Earth year, each Martian season is about twice as long as it would be on Earth. On Mars, you would have to keep your winter clothes out for a long time—the cold Martian winter lasts about six months.

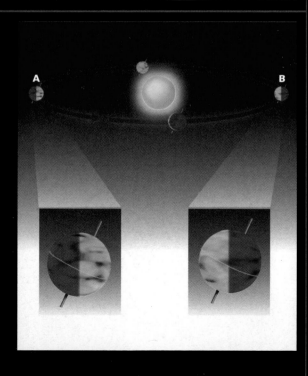

In 1877, an Italian astronomer named Giovanni Schiaparelli turned his telescope toward Mars. He described features on the surface as *canali,* the Italian word for "channels," but his description was incorrectly translated into English as "canals." Soon astronomers from around the world, looking at a blurry Mars, were sketching maps showing long, straight "canals" criss-crossing the planet's surface. But their imaginations were creating patterns in the blurry images that were not really there.

The most famous of these astronomers was an American named Percival Lowell. He drew very detailed sketches of what he believed he saw on the surface of Mars. He also developed a theory that the long canals were built by intelligent Martians, who were trying to save their planet from a terrible drought by pumping water from the polar regions to the dry farmland near the equator.

Few scientists shared this view. But Lowell wrote about his ideas in magazines and newspapers, and by the early 1900s much of the public had heard about Lowell's race of intelligent Martians and their system of water canals.

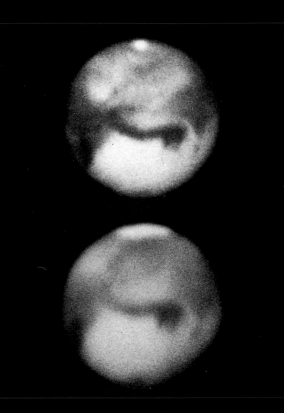

→ *Mars looked blurry through early telescopes. But astronomers could see the light and dark areas change with the seasons.*

↓ *This map was made in the early 1960s. It was the most accurate map of Mars before spacecraft surveyed the planet.*

↑ *Percival Lowell sketched several globes of Mars. This one,*

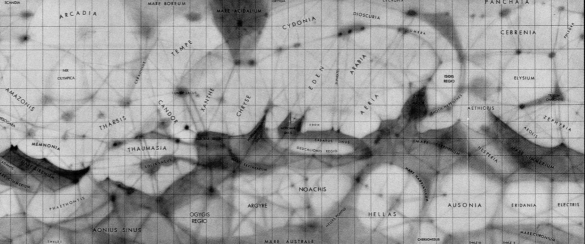

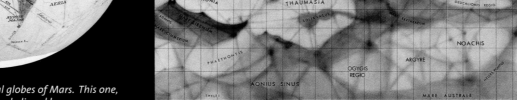

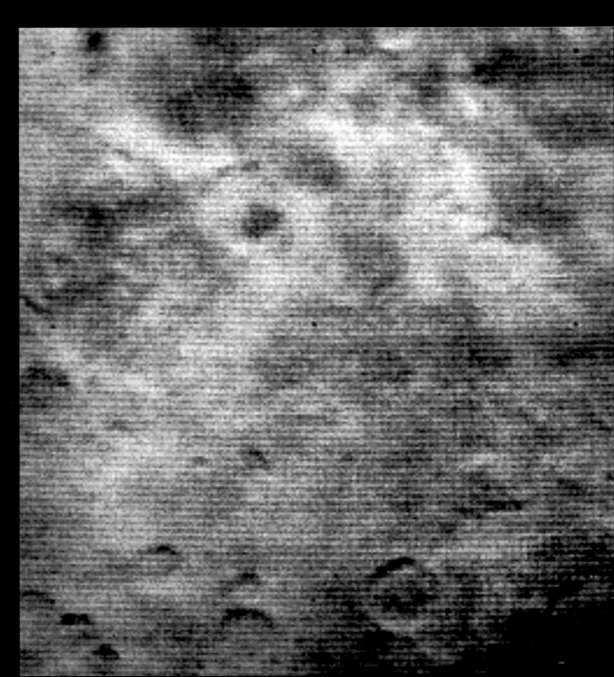

Over the years, telescopes became better and better. But the telescopes were viewing a planet millions of miles away and could not see the Martian surface clearly. By the early 1960s, the most accurate globe of Mars still showed very little detail and even included a few straight lines that looked a lot like Lowell's canals.

But space exploration was just beginning. In 1965, the *Mariner 4* spacecraft flew past Mars and sent back the first close-up photographs of its surface. The photos showed no vegetation, no canals, and no water. Overnight, our view of Mars changed.

↑ *The* Mariner 4 *spacecraft.*

→ *One of the 22 photographs taken by the* Mariner 4 *spacecraft as it flew past Mars. This was the first photograph clearly showing craters on the Martian surface.*

No person has ever set foot on the Red Planet. Most of what we know about Mars we have learned by sending robot spacecraft on one-way trips to that faraway world.

The first spacecraft flew past Mars, transmitting information to Earth as they zipped by. Later spacecraft went into orbit around Mars. As they circled the planet, they sent pictures and data millions of miles back to Earth. Only a few space-craft have actually landed on Mars. Acting as our remote senses, they have sniffed the Martian air, gazed at Martian rocks, and sifted through Martian soil.

The spacecraft circling Mars have sent back thousands and thousands of photographs. From these photographs, scientists have pieced together a detailed mosaic of the planet's surface.

Even at a glance, it is obvious that Mars is very different from Earth. When you compare pictures of the two planets, the first thing you notice is that Earth is covered with sparkling blue water. Mars has none. There are no Martian oceans. There are no rivers or lakes. There is no liquid water on the surface at all.

Earth and Mars, to scale.

This is an important difference. It is water that makes Earth a living planet, different from all the other planets in the solar system, including Mars.

The next thing you notice is that Mars is red. Close-up views of the surface show us that "the Red Planet" is a good name for this place. The rusty red color comes from iron in the Martian soil. Mars' rocky plains are covered with red soil, and a fine red dust is everywhere.

The photographs also show similarities between the two planets. Mars, like Earth, has permanent icecaps at its north and south poles. These are the coldest parts of the planet because sunlight strikes the equator more directly than it strikes the poles. Mars' north pole is mostly water ice, covered by carbon dioxide ice in the winter. Its south pole probably also has water ice, but it is topped by a permanent layer of carbon dioxide ice. The icecaps grow in the fall as the temperature drops, then shrink in the spring when the weather warms.

MARS GLOBAL SURVEYOR

Back in the days of Schiaparelli and Lowell, maps of Mars were drawn by hand. Astronomers squinted through telescopes and sketched the fuzzy features that they saw. Now, a century later, the mountains, craters, and canyons on Mars are being charted in accurate detail by orbiting spacecraft. Mars Global Surveyor began mapping the planet in 1999. As it circles above, its high-resolution camera snaps photographs of the surface below.

Meanwhile, the spacecraft's laser altimeter charts the highs and lows of the planet's surface. This instrument measures elevation by beaming laser pulses down to the ground, then timing how long it takes them to bounce back up to the spacecraft. Scientists are combining the images and surface heights to make the first accurate global map of Mars. The map will provide valuable scientific information and will be used to select landing sites for future spacecraft.

Artist's rendering of the Mars Global Surveyor *in orbit around Mars.*

Like Earth, Mars has breathtaking volcanic mountains and deep valleys. But on Mars these features are much grander in scale. Mars has the largest volcanoes and the longest, deepest canyons in the entire solar system. Enormous volcanic peaks poke up through the high Martian clouds; huge fractures in the crust stretch for thousands of miles. Earth's mountains are tiny by comparison, and its canyons are nothing more than small cracks.

These gigantic volcanoes and canyons tell scientists that Mars is an active planet. Though much of its surface hasn't changed for billions of years, part of it has been pushed and stretched by forces deep underground. On one side of the planet, a huge region has been pushed up from below and now bulges six miles above the rest of Mars. This vast area, called the Tharsis region, is nearly the size of North America.

Tharsis is home to hundreds of Martian volcanoes. Rising just off its western edge is Olympus Mons, the largest mountain in the solar system. This enormous volcano, which would cover the entire state of Arizona, is more than 16 miles high—three times higher than Mount Everest, the tallest mountain on Earth. Though it is possible that some Martian volcanoes are still active, no eruptions have ever been observed. Most took place billions of years ago, when Mars was very young.

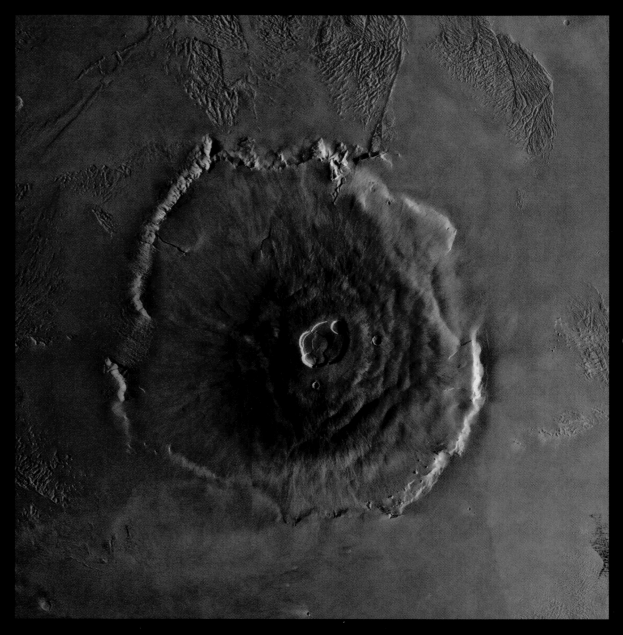

This image, looking straight down on Olympus Mons, was pieced together from several Viking photographs. The base of the volcano is nearly 400 miles across.

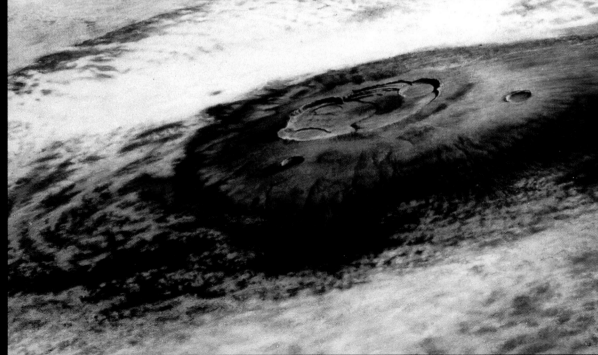

The map image shows labels: ARCADIA PLANITIA, ACIDALIA PLANITIA, ALBA PATERA, TEMPE, TERRA, CHRYSE, AMAZONIS, PLANITIA, OLYMPUS MONS, LUNAE, PLANITIA, PLANUM, XANTHE, TERRA, THARSIS MONTES, MARGARITIFER TERRA, SYRIA PLANUM, SINAI PLANUM, PLANITIA, OLYMPUS MONS, 10 miles, ↓ sea level, MAUNA LOA

↑ Olympus Mons is much larger than Mauna Loa in Hawaii, the largest volcano on Earth.

← Map showing Olympus Mons and a line of three other huge volcanoes in the Tharsis region (the Tharsis Montes: Arsia Mons, Pavonis Mons, and Ascraeus Mons). The map also shows Valles Marineris and Chryse Planitia, the region where both Pathfinder and Viking 1 landed.

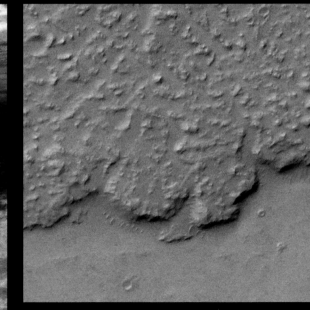

↑ The edge of a huge lava flow southwest of Arsia Mons, a large volcano in the Tharsis region. (Mars Global Surveyor)

← Olympus Mons rises above the Martian clouds. (Viking)

The bulging Tharsis region has split and cracked in many places, creating networks of deep fractures. Valles Marineris (Mariner Valley, named after the *Mariner* spacecraft that first photographed it) is like a big gash in the planet. This huge valley is the longest and the deepest in the solar system. Valles Marineris would stretch all the way across the United States, from the Pacific Ocean in the west to the Atlantic Ocean in the east.

The entire Grand Canyon would fit in one of its small side canyons. If a Martian rock tumbled off the rim of Valles Marineris, it would fall four miles before hitting the canyon floor.

→ *Valles Marineris stretches across the middle of the planet. Two of the Tharsis volcanoes, Pavonis Mons and Ascraeus Mons, are visible on the far left.*

↓ *A computer-generated image, looking down Valles Marineris.*

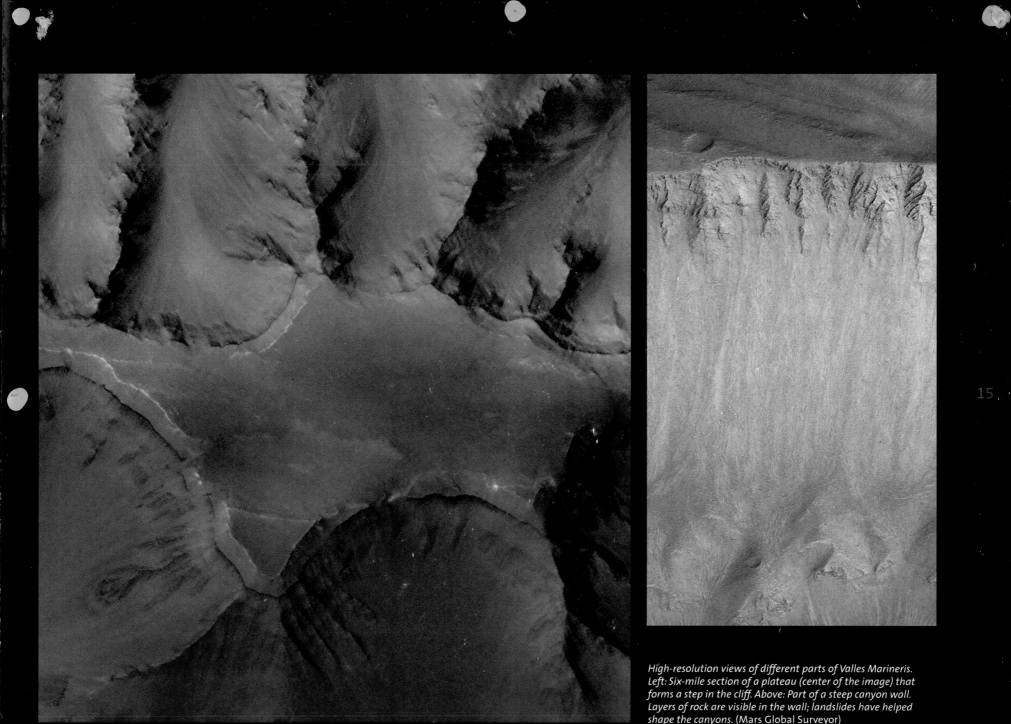

15

High-resolution views of different parts of Valles Marineris. Left: Six-mile section of a plateau (center of the image) that forms a step in the cliff. Above: Part of a steep canyon wall. Layers of rock are visible in the wall; landslides have helped shape the canyons. (Mars Global Surveyor)

Photographs of Mars show that much of the planet is covered with craters. Early in the history of our solar system, Mars, Earth, and the other planets were bombarded by meteors that blasted craters in their surfaces. Most of Earth's craters have been erased. Some have been eroded away by water, some buried as the land has changed, and some hidden by vegetation. But Mars still shows the scars of thousands of these violent collisions. The largest is the Hellas Basin, a huge depression that is 1,300 miles across and six miles deep. This crater, which resulted from a truly planet-jarring collision long ago, would cover nearly half the United States.

Four billion years ago, all of Mars was probably covered with craters. Since then, much of the land north of Mars' equator has been flooded by lava flowing from the volcanoes in the Tharsis region and elsewhere. Many of the old impact craters in the north have been covered over, buried by lava.

In contrast, the southern part of Mars is still carpeted in craters. This part of the planet has not been resurfaced by flowing lava. The heavily cratered land in the south is nearly four billion years old and has changed very little during that time.

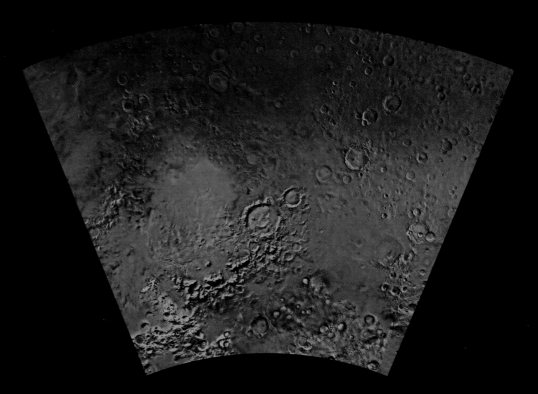

↑ *The heavily cratered Martian highlands. The circular light-colored area is the Argyre impact basin, a crater nearly 500 miles across that is surrounded by a rim of rugged mountains. (Viking)*

↓ *Not many of Earth's impact craters are still visible. The Manicouagan Crater in Quebec, Canada, was formed 200 million years ago and is now heavily eroded. Though small compared to Argyre, it is almost 45 miles across.*

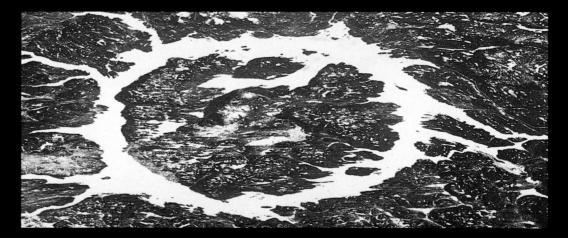

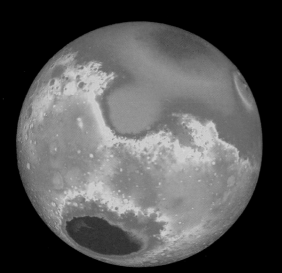

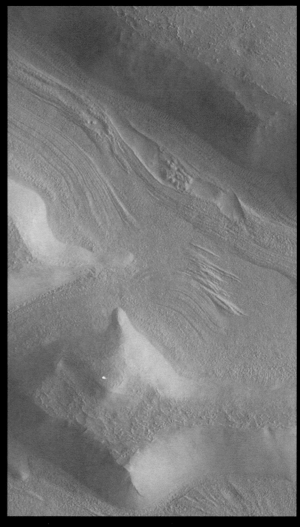

↑ *These maps of Mars were made from millions of elevation measurements taken by Mars Global Surveyor. The colors represent the different heights of the surface. The lowest parts of the planet are purple and blue; the highest parts are white and red. Mars has the highest, the lowest, and the smoothest* land in the solar system. Above left: The huge Hellas Basin (the large dark blue circle), surrounded by countless smaller craters. Above right: The Tharsis region with its large volcanoes (white) and Valles Marineris (horizontal green gash). The largest volcano is Olympus Mons.

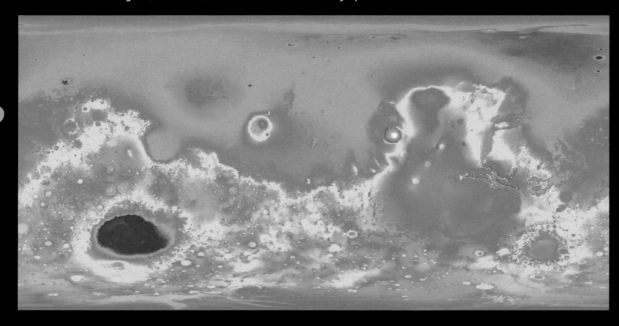

↑ *This steep-walled valley with its grooved floor is part of a region of mesas and canyons that separates the highlands in the south from the lowlands in the north. (Mars Global Surveyor)*

← *The flat map shows the dramatic difference between the northern and southern parts of the planet. The south is high and scarred with craters; the north is about three miles lower and very smooth. Why is the north so smooth? Part of it has been paved over by lava, and part may once have been covered by oceans.*

In 1976 *Viking 1* and *Viking 2* settled softly onto the surface of Mars. They were the first spacecraft from Earth ever to visit the Red Planet. Twenty-one years later, *Pathfinder* dropped out of the Martian sky to join them. A parachute opened to slow it down, then giant air bags inflated to cushion it during impact. *Pathfinder* bounced hard more than 15 times before it rolled to a stop on the red Martian soil.

Although the *Viking* and *Pathfinder* landers arrived at different locations, they landed in similar terrain. Engineers did not want to risk landing these precious spacecraft on the edge of a cliff or the side of a volcano. They guided them to different sites on the gently rolling Martian plains north of the equator. The pictures the spacecraft sent back showed flat, windswept landscapes strewn with gray rocks and covered with fine red dust.

Pathfinder landed in Ares Vallis, an ancient floodplain. Many of the rocks here were deposited by floods billions of years ago. This panorama also shows Pathfinder's *deflated air bags and the ramp that its small rover,* Sojourner, *drove down to reach the surface. The rover is analyzing a rock a few feet from the lander. When* Sojourner *rolled down* Pathfinder's *ramp, it became the first rover ever to explore the Martian surface.*

← *The* Pathfinder *lander. When the air bags that had protected it deflated,* Pathfinder *opened like a flower to reveal a camera, a weather station, and its rover,* Sojourner. *This photograph was taken by* Sojourner *after it had left the lander. The camera, at the top of the mast, is looking at* Sojourner.

The two *Viking* landers could not move from their landing sites. They could reach out only a few feet with their robot arms to scoop up small samples of soil. *Pathfinder* carried the first rover to Mars. The rover, *Sojourner*, was about the size of a small dog. *Sojourner* traveled on six rugged wheels at the end of flexible legs. It moved at a snail's pace, but was able to travel several yards from the lander.

The little robot geologist dug its wheels into the red Martian dirt, churning up the soil to analyze its texture and clumpiness. It roamed through a garden of nearby rocks, ranging in size from pebbles to boulders, and nuzzled up to several of them.

The Martian rocks and soil seem to be made of about the same minerals, though in different proportions, as the rocks and soil on Earth.

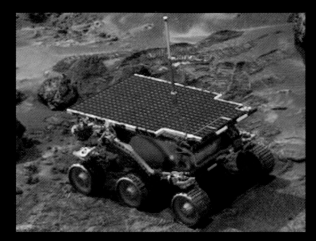

→ *Sojourner had TV cameras for eyes and was steered by drivers back on Earth.* (Pathfinder)

This dry, dusty world does not look very hospitable. But many scientists have wondered whether there might be microscopic life on its surface. The *Viking* landers performed three important experiments that scientists hoped would answer that question. Their long robot arms scooped up samples of Martian soil and carried them inside the landers, where instruments analyzed the red dirt for evidence of life.

In planning these experiments, scientists assumed that Martian microbes would be similar to those on Earth: they would take in food molecules, grow, and release waste molecules. In one experiment, nutrients were added to soil samples. Then an instrument looked for the waste gas carbon dioxide, which might signal that living organisms had eaten the food.

This experiment did not find evidence of Martian life. Results from the other two experiments were also negative.

But are the building blocks of life present in the Martian soil? Another experiment looked for organic molecules, the molecules that make up living things. Samples of soil were heated, and instruments watched for gases that would be released if organic molecules were present. It was a great surprise when none were found. Scientists know that meteorites and interplanetary dust deliver a steady supply of organic molecules to the Martian surface. So even if there are no living organisms, there should still be some organic molecules. Scientists now suspect that they are being destroyed by harsh chemicals present in the Martian soil.

Spacecraft that have followed *Viking* have not carried experiments to look for evidence of life. The few *Viking* experiments are all scientists have to go by. Most scientists do not believe that there is life on the surface of Mars today. But many believe it is possible that primitive life exists beneath the surface, or that life existed on the planet long ago.

← *Sojourner's cameras took these close-up pictures of interesting rocks in the Rock Garden. Right: A rock named Chimp, with small pebbles and wind streaks in the foreground. Left: A pitted rock named Half-Dome. It looks as if it has been sandblasted by the Martian winds.*

→ *The* Viking 2 *lander's robot arm scoops up a sample of soil and leaves its mark in the ground.*

Earth is surrounded by an atmosphere that protects all the plants and animals on the planet from the extreme conditions in space. It shields us from the sun's radiation, helps keep our planet warm, and contains the oxygen that many of Earth's creatures need to survive.

Mars, too, has an atmosphere, but it is very different from Earth's. The Martian atmosphere is very, very thin and is made up almost entirely of carbon dioxide. Fine red Martian dust fills the thin air and creates a pink sky all year round.

Each of the landers set up a small weather station on the surface of Mars. While the stations operated, they radioed weather reports to Earth. Like the weather on Earth, the weather on Mars changes from day to day and from season to season. On some days the pink sky is mostly sunny, with light winds and wispy rose-colored clouds. On other days the sky is overcast, with strong winds and swirling cinnamon-colored dust.

↗ *Space shuttle astronauts took this picture of Earth's atmosphere at sunset. Storm clouds rise about eight miles above the planet's surface.*

→ *An unusually clear view of the Martian atmosphere. Thin layers of haze extend 25 miles above the horizon. (Viking)*

The weather reports never included rain. There is very little water vapor in the Martian atmosphere. Martian clouds contain crystals of water ice, but the air is too thin and too cold for raindrops to form. In the early mornings, a thin veil of fog might fill the distant canyons, but there is no dew on the canyon walls. The rain that nourishes all life on Earth never falls on Mars.

23

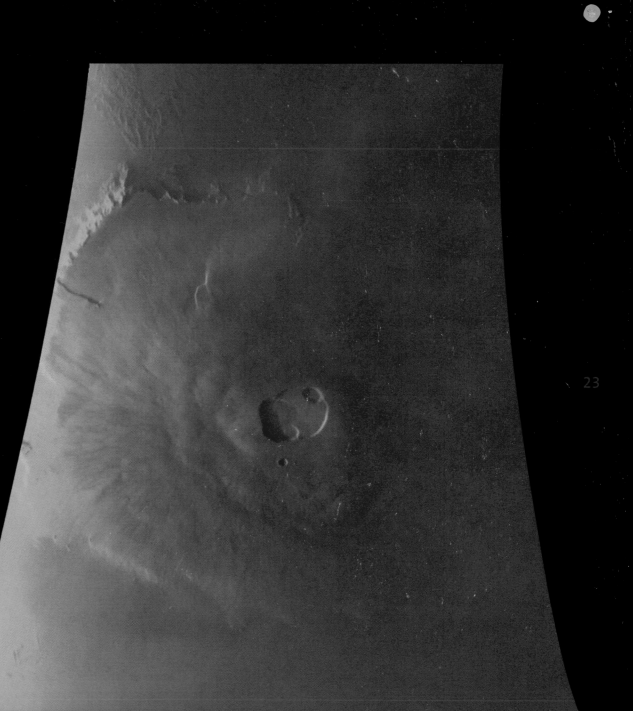

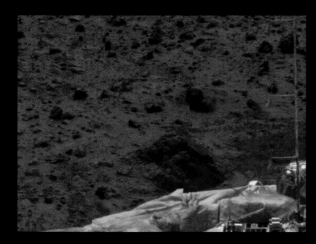

↑ Pathfinder's *weather station. The windsocks on the far right are slightly tilted because they are being blown by the Martian wind.*

→ *During the late afternoon, clouds accumulate around and above Olympus Mons. (Mars Global Surveyor)*

The air on Mars is very thin. Because it is so thin, water cannot exist as a liquid on Mars' surface. If an astronaut on Mars poured a glass of water, it would soon boil away.

The boiling point of water (the temperature at which it turns into a gas) depends on the pressure of the surrounding air. You can see this yourself if you go camping in the mountains. Near sea level, water has to be heated to 212 degrees Fahrenheit before it will boil. As you climb up a mountain, the air gets thinner and thinner, so water boils at a lower and lower temperature. On a 5,000-foot-high mountain (and in the mile-high city of Denver), water boils at about 203 degrees Fahrenheit (a few degrees lower than at sea level). At the top of Mount Everest, the highest mountain on Earth, water boils at only about 160 degrees Fahrenheit.

When spacecraft measured the air pressure on the surface of Mars, they found that it is the same as it would be on a mountain more than three times as high as Mount Everest. When the air is that thin, water boils at very low temperatures—temperatures near its freezing point. That means that water on Mars exists either as ice or as water vapor (a gas), but not as a liquid.

Mars is very, very cold. Even on bright summer days, temperatures may only reach 10 degrees Fahrenheit—22 degrees below the freezing point of water. When the sun goes down, the temperature falls to a frigid 110 degrees below zero. Earth's atmosphere helps keep our planet warm overnight. But on Mars the atmosphere is so thin that after the sun sets, the planet's heat quickly escapes to space.

If you were standing on Mars on a summer morning, your feet would be warm, but your ears would be freezing! As the sun warms the soil, the air a few inches above the ground is heated to nearly 50 degrees Fahrenheit. But just a few feet off the ground, the temperature plummets.

Winters on Mars are so cold that nearly 20 percent of the planet's air actually freezes out of the sky. Carbon dioxide gas in the air turns to ice and is trapped in Mars' polar icecaps until spring. Then when the temperature warms, the carbon dioxide goes back into the air as a gas.

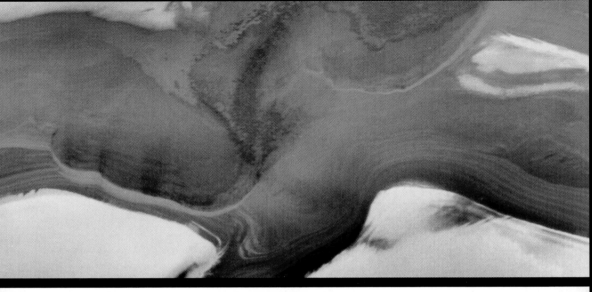

↗ *A section of the north polar cap. Layers of white ice and reddish orange dust form terraces around both the north and south polar caps.* (Viking)

→ *Frost covers the Martian landscape near the* Viking 2 *landing site in Utopia Planitia in the Elysium region.*

← *Wispy clouds about 10 miles high, made of water ice condensed on particles of red dust.* (Pathfinder)

Mars is a windy planet. Dust devils whirl across the surface, lifting red dust high into the sky. During some parts of the year, ferocious winds stir up huge dust storms in the Southern Hemisphere that can grow to cover the entire planet. These dust storms are far worse than any on Earth and can completely block our view of the planet's surface for weeks at a time.

Over the ages, Martian winds have created complex sand dunes over much of the planet. Some dunes appear to be ancient remnants of an earlier time when the air was thicker and the wind could more easily blow sand around. Other dunes appear to be still active today.

→ *The north polar cap is surrounded by sand dunes. These dunes look bright because a layer of white frost covers the red sand. (Mars Global Surveyor)*

↓ *Sand dunes like these cover much of Mars. (Mars Global Surveyor)*

↓ *Sand dunes are also common on Earth. These dunes in Algeria were photographed by astronauts in the space shuttle.*

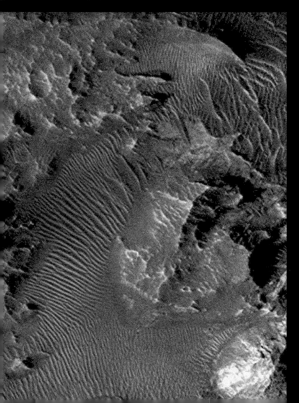

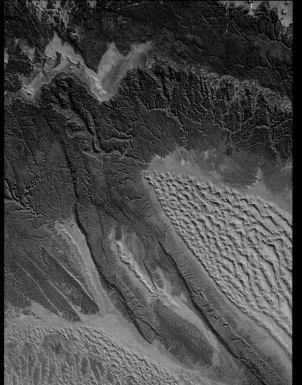

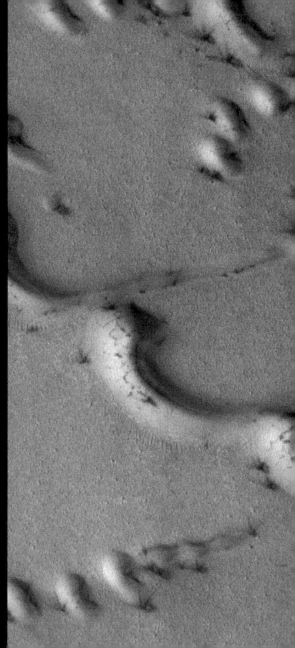

When the first astronauts visit Mars, what will they find? Though an astronaut could not survive without a spacesuit, she would feel more at home on Mars than anywhere else in the solar system. She could stand on a rocky surface, scoop up a gloveful of dirt, and explore extinct volcanoes and ancient canyons.

She would need the spacesuit to protect her from the thin Martian air and the extreme cold. The spacesuit would be bulky, but not heavy. Because Mars is smaller than Earth, the pull of gravity on its surface is lower. She and her spacesuit would weigh about one-third what they weighed on Earth.

As the astronaut hiked across the rugged, rocky terrain, her boots would leave deep footprints in the dusty red soil. Fine red dust would cling to her spacesuit. Even on days when the wind was calm, she would look up at a pink sky loaded with red dust. As she headed back to the warmth of her spacecraft at the end of the day, she would look past the silhouettes of crater rims at a dimmer setting sun.

The planet she was exploring would seem strangely familiar. But it would be missing the air and water that make Earth habitable, and the plants and animals that share her home world.

A Martian sunset.

Mars is a dry, desolate planet.

But the same photographs that show us the dry desert of today also let us look back in time, giving us a glimpse of an earlier Mars. The old, cratered terrain is etched with dry riverbeds, suggesting that water once flowed on the planet's surface. Today the air is far too thin, and far too cold, for streams to flow in the Martian valleys. But 3.8 billion years ago, when Mars was young, there was water. Ancient Mars was very different from the planet that now twinkles in our night sky.

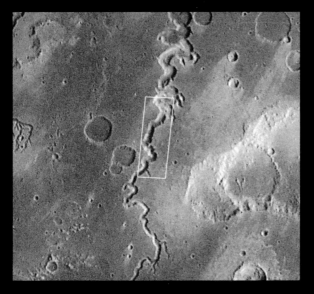

Both Viking *and* Mars Global Surveyor *photographed this Martian valley cutting through a region in the cratered southern highlands. Mars Global Surveyor's higher-resolution view (right) was the first to show a small inner channel (at the top of the photo). This inner channel suggests that a steady flow of water may have cut the valley. This is the way that many river valleys are formed on Earth.*

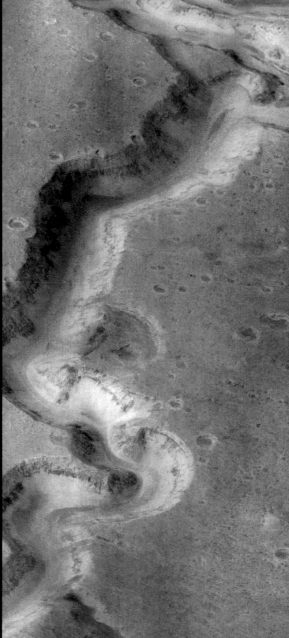

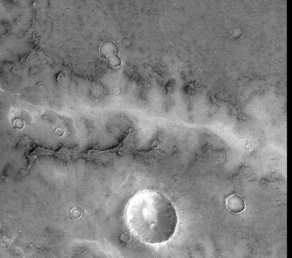

Top: This photograph shows narrow branching valleys winding between craters in the southern highlands. Some may have been created as rainwater formed small streams that came together and grew into larger and larger streams. (Viking)

Bottom: A closer view of a small portion of another branching valley. (Mars Global Surveyor)

Mars and Earth formed at about the same time, about 4.5 billion years ago. Before then, our entire solar system was just a huge rotating cloud of gas and dust. Then the cloud began to collapse. Its center shrank to form our sun. As it contracted, the sun heated up until the temperature and pressure at its center were high enough for colliding hydrogen atoms to combine to form helium. This process releases enormous amounts of energy and is the source of the sunlight that bathes our solar system. The sun began to shine.

Eventually, the rotating cloud of gas surrounding the early sun began to cool and condense into very small, solid particles. These tiny pieces of rock and ice stuck together when they collided, and slowly grew to the size of pebbles, then baseballs, and then boulders. They continued to collide and combine, growing into larger and larger objects called planetesimals. Eventually, a few of the planetesimals swept up the smaller ones in their paths and grew to become the planets.

Earth and Mars formed out of this flurry of planetesimals. At first, the two planets were so hot that they were molten. Slowly, the rock near their surfaces cooled and formed their first solid crusts. But the interiors of the two planets were still intensely hot. Volcanoes punched through the crust, spewing red-hot lava everywhere.

Steam and other hot gases bubbled out through cracks in the surface and erupted from young volcanoes to form the early atmospheres of Earth and Mars. The air on the two planets was thick, consisting mostly of carbon dioxide, water vapor, and nitrogen—nothing like the air we now breathe on Earth, or the air that our space-craft have sampled on Mars.

Early Earth and Mars were constantly bombarded by leftover planetesimals and icy comets. They battered the planets and scarred their land with thousands of craters. But they also brought more ice and rock to the two young worlds. About four billion years ago, this heavy bombardment began to ease up, giving the young planets a chance to evolve.

No one knows for sure what Earth and Mars were like so long ago. But early Earth was probably turbulent, warm, and wet. As its atmosphere cooled, dark clouds filled its skies. The water vapor in the air condensed into water droplets, and torrential rain poured down on the planet. Streams and rivers cut through the rugged land, and water flooded the low basins, forming the first oceans.

Four billion years ago, Mars was proba-bly much warmer than it is today, but still cooler than its neighbor. In the chilly, thick Martian atmosphere, carbon dioxide con-densed to form ice crystals. Clouds of this

ice may have filled the early Martian skies. Though these clouds would have blocked much of the faint sunlight, they could also have acted like a blanket for the planet, trapping its heat and warming the surface.

In the colder parts of the planet, storms may have unleashed blizzards of snow and carbon dioxide ice. In warmer regions, there

may have been occasional rain, which collected in cool streams and icy lakes. We don't know how warm early Mars was, but we know that it was around this time that many of the ancient Martian riverbeds carried water.

An early planet, as it might have looked about 4.4 billion years ago. This planet could be either Earth or Mars at that time.

As the young Earth cooled, its crust broke into several enormous pieces, called plates. The plates carry the continents and float on a sea of molten rock. Their motion gradually changes Earth's surface. They inch along ever so slowly, relentlessly rearranging the continents and oceans. As they collide, they drive part of the crust down into Earth's molten interior and recycle its rock.

Mars is a smaller planet, so it cooled more quickly than Earth. Though its earliest crust may have broken into plates, as the planet cooled its crust thickened. Mars soon became a one-plate planet. Still, its hot interior was active. The Tharsis bulge was pushed up by molten rock, and Mars' enormous volcanoes were all driven by heat from below.

Earth is still a very active planet. Earthquakes and volcanic eruptions, caused by the motion of the plates, occur every day. Mars began with less internal heat than its larger neighbor, and it lost its heat more quickly. As its heat engine slowed down, the planet's hot interior had less and less effect on its surface. Most of the southern half of Mars hasn't changed in nearly four billion years.

Earth's ancient atmosphere gradually began to change. The carbon dioxide was slowly removed from the air and stored in its oceans and land. Early torrential rainstorms carried this gas, dissolved in raindrops, down to the ground. Some splashed in the early oceans. Some rained onto the land, dissolving rock as it trickled over it. The dissolved chemicals could then recombine to make new rock, called carbonate rock. This process takes carbon dioxide that was once in the atmosphere and traps it in rock.

Some of this carbon dioxide eventually returns to the atmosphere. As Earth's plates move, rock is driven down into the planet's hot interior. When the molten rock rises again through volcanoes, carbon dioxide bubbles back out into the air.

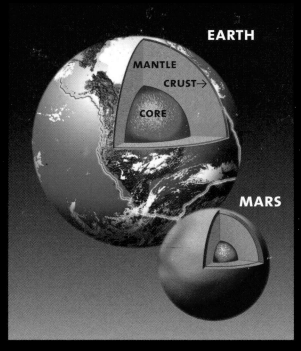

EARTH

MANTLE

CRUST→

CORE

MARS

Both Earth and Mars have solid cores surrounded by a molten mantle of liquid rock and a thin rocky crust. Mars is a smaller planet. It cooled more quickly and has a smaller core and a thicker crust.

Mars' atmosphere changed too. Carbon dioxide may have been gradually pulled from the atmosphere to the land, just as it was on Earth. Some might have come down dissolved in Martian rain. As on Earth, the carbon dioxide in water would dissolve bits of rock, then combine with these minerals to form carbonate rock. Some of the carbon dioxide may have come down in ice storms and formed ice sheets like those at the poles.

Early in its history, while volcanic activity was common, Mars was able to add some carbon dioxide back to the atmosphere. But eventually, as its internal heat engine slowed down, this process nearly stopped.

Also, because Mars is smaller than Earth, it did not have quite as tight a grip on its atmosphere. The lightest gases could escape Mars' gravitational pull more easily than they could Earth's. As sunlight struck molecules high in Mars' atmosphere, it broke some of them apart into atoms. Those atoms could then drift away into space. For example, nitrogen remained in Earth's atmosphere but was slowly, atom by atom, able to escape from Mars' atmosphere.

Mars lost some of its atmosphere to space, and some became locked in the land. If Mars had been the same size as Earth, it might still have a thick atmosphere. Instead, it now has very little of its original atmosphere left.

Life first appeared on our planet shortly after Earth's crust formed. Fossils of primitive microscopic cells date back 3.5 billion years. There is even some evidence that life may have existed as early as 3.9 billion years ago.

How could life begin on such a violent, stormy, meteor-battered planet? Amazingly, life has only a few basic needs—water, organic molecules, and an energy source. Each of these was plentiful on the young Earth.

Water is essential to life. It makes up about two-thirds of every living thing, from bacteria and butterflies to earthworms and elephants. The watery environment inside cells is where all the chemical reactions take place that keep living things alive. Water covered Earth long ago, just as it does today.

The elements carbon, hydrogen, nitrogen, and oxygen are also vital. These are the most common elements in the solar system. Simple molecules, made of combinations of these atoms, were abundant in the waters of early Earth. Then some form of energy—maybe sunlight, lightning, or heat from inside the planet—caused these elements to combine into more complex "organic" molecules, the molecules that make up living things.

Over time, the first living organisms formed out of the brew of organic molecules in the waters of Earth. These were microscopic living things that were able to reproduce themselves from the organic molecules in their environment. But this process was not perfect. By chance, some organisms were better able to compete for the necessary organic molecules than others. Evolution had begun.

No one knows for sure when or where the first cells formed. But scientists think there were several places on early Earth where life could have begun. It may have started in muddy tide pools, where organic molecules collected as they washed ashore with the tide. It may have started on the ocean floor, where organic molecules settled out of the waters near volcanic vents. It may have started in volcanic hot springs, where the rising water was enriched with minerals as it gushed toward the surface.

The earliest forms of recognizable life were tiny single cells that resemble today's bacteria. And for most of Earth's history—until about 500 million years ago—our planet was inhabited only by these microscopic organisms, which are much too small to see. For more than three billion years, life on Earth was invisible. Earth's surface must have looked as barren as the Martian landscape does today.

→ Painting of Earth as it might have looked about 3.8 to 4 billion years ago. The inset shows some of the simple molecules that were in the waters of early Earth. These simple molecules can combine to form complex organic molecules. Organic molecules make up all living things, including these primitive microscopic cells.

↓ Earth time line from 4.5 billion years ago to the present, showing the approximate times of some important periods in Earth's evolution.

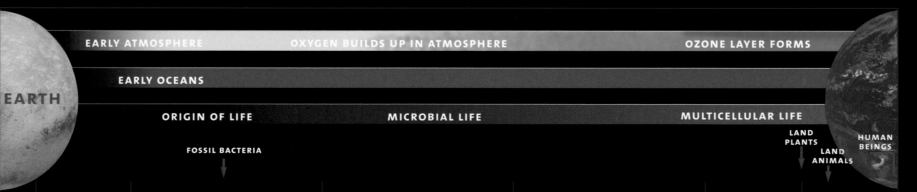

EARTH

EARLY ATMOSPHERE   OXYGEN BUILDS UP IN ATMOSPHERE   OZONE LAYER FORMS

EARLY OCEANS

ORIGIN OF LIFE   MICROBIAL LIFE   MULTICELLULAR LIFE

FOSSIL BACTERIA

LAND PLANTS   HUMAN BEINGS
LAND ANIMALS

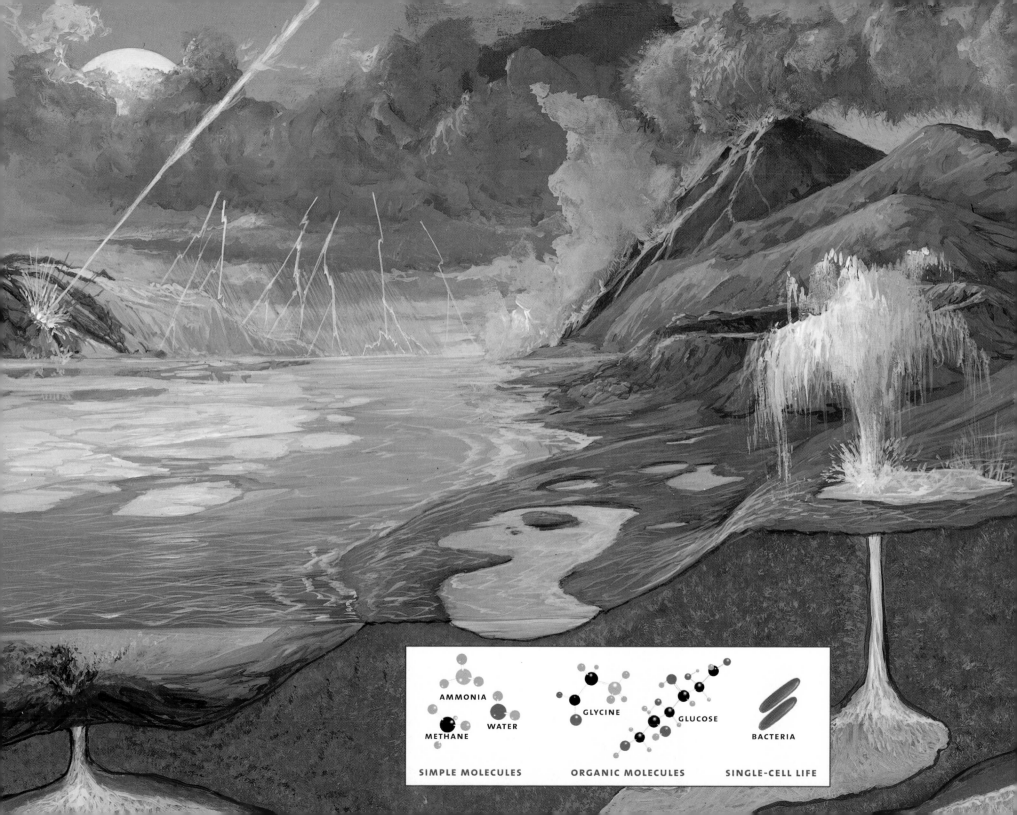

SIMPLE MOLECULES

ORGANIC MOLECULES

SINGLE-CELL LIFE

AMMONIA

METHANE

WATER

GLYCINE

GLUCOSE

BACTERIA

About four billion years ago, ancient Mars may have been similar to ancient Earth. Could life have started there too?

For life to begin, there has to be water. Some of the photographs taken by spacecraft show dry riverbeds on the Martian surface. About 3.8 billion years ago, when these riverbeds were formed, there was water on Mars. Back then, the Martian canyons may have been filled with chilly water. The southern highlands may have been dotted with icy crater lakes. And geysers near volcanic hot springs may have sprayed water high into the Martian sky.

Carbon, hydrogen, nitrogen, and oxygen—the elements that combine to form organic molecules—were abundant in the early solar system. They were also delivered to the young planet by icy comets and wayward planetesimals that pelted its surface. These basic elements would have been present in the waters of early Mars, just as they were in the waters of early Earth.

Mars also had energy sources that could have triggered the building of organic molecules from simpler molecules in the water. Molten lava churned below the rocky surface and erupted through volcanoes and cracks in the ground. Bolts of lightning may have crackled in the Martian sky. Dim but powerful sunlight fell on the Martian surface.

Although Mars was a smaller, more distant world, life could have started there just as it started on Earth. Many of the same watery habitats that could have nurtured life on Earth may also have existed on Mars. Life may have started at the bottom of a Martian lake, where organic molecules collected in the muddy red sediments. Or it may have started in volcanic hot springs, like those in Earth's frigid Arctic, where steaming waters rise to the surface through the frozen ground. Given enough time, organic molecules circulating in these Martian waters could have formed primitive organisms.

But was there enough time? The conditions on the planet quickly began to change.

As Mars' atmosphere began to thin, more of its heat escaped to space. For a while, temperatures sometimes rose above freezing during the day. Ice-covered lakes may still have held water, insulated by the layer of ice above or warmed by heat from below. Eventually, though, Mars' atmosphere became so thin, and its temperature so cold, that all of the water disappeared from its surface. Gone were the icy lakes, the water-filled canyons, and the muddy red rivers. If life did begin on early Mars, could it survive?

→ Painting of Mars as it might have looked about 3.8 to 4 billion years ago. The inset shows some of the simple molecules that were in the waters of early Mars. Did life evolve on Mars too?

↓ Mars time line from 4.5 billion years ago to the present, showing the approximate times of some important periods in Mars' evolution.

MARS

EARLY ATMOSPHERE

EARLY SURFACE WATER   OCCASIONAL FLOODS   UNDERGROUND WATER?

?   ORIGIN OF LIFE?   MICROBIAL LIFE?

4.5   4   3   2   now

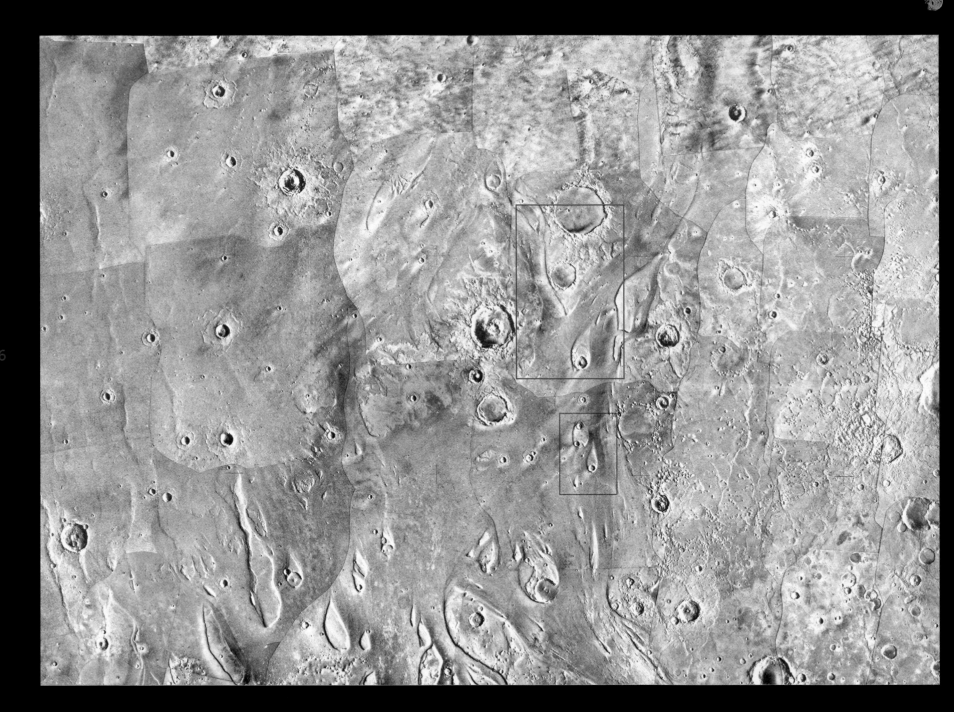

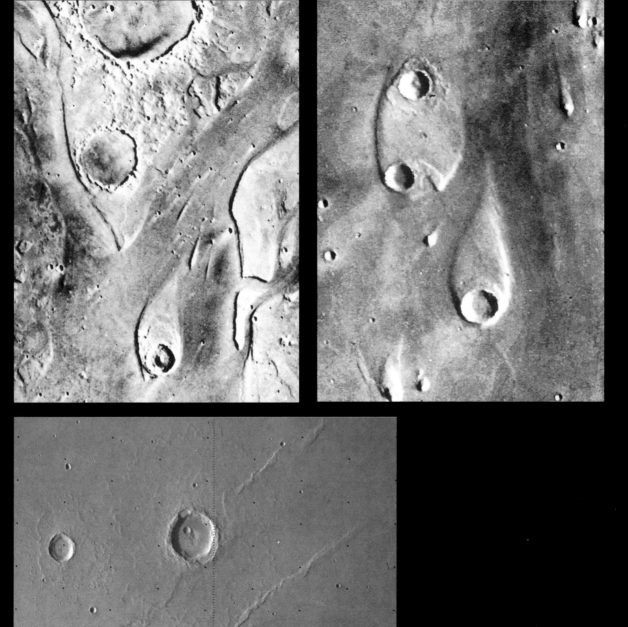

← *This photo mosaic shows the ancient Martian floodplain where Ares Vallis joins Chryse Planitia. The floodwaters rushed from bottom to top across the middle of the picture. The* Pathfinder *spacecraft landed in this region.* (Viking)

→ *Close-ups of landforms in the picture on the facing page. Left: Rushing water carved streamlined islands where it encountered obstacles, like crater rims. Right: The teardrop-shaped island is nearly 30 miles long and about 2,000 feet high—as tall as a small mountain on Earth. Its crater is over six miles across.* (Viking)

Even after water vanished from its surface, Mars was still a water-rich planet. Some water was frozen at the poles, but most of it appears to have been hidden underground. Evidence of this comes from spacecraft photographs. They show deep channels and teardrop-shaped islands that were carved by catastrophic floods that swept across the Martian lands. Some of these floods occurred long after the water had vanished from the planet's surface. Scientists believe that impacts by large meteors or heat from rising molten lava suddenly melted ice beneath the ground, releasing giant waves of water.

Over the years, there were several great Martian floods. This means that a huge amount of water or ice was stored below the surface. It may have been miles down, perhaps in huge reservoirs capped by a thick layer of ice. It may have been trapped in porous underground rock that soaked up water like a sponge.

→ *It looks as if this meteor impact melted frozen water beneath the surface.* (Viking)

Martian microbes, if they did exist, might have survived underground, in places where there was still water. Primitive organisms are very hardy. Life thrives in some of the most unlikely places on Earth. Colonies of bacteria live in sandstone rock in the frigid deserts of Antarctica; others live in the boiling-hot waters of Old Faithful in Yellowstone National Park; and still others live in almost-solid rock, miles beneath Earth's surface.

Some Martian microbes might have lived in similar, seemingly hostile, environments. Maybe they lived miles deep, in water heated by scalding volcanic vents; maybe they lived nearer the surface, in the moist cracks of rock fractured by meteor impacts. If primitive life did begin on Mars, it had a chance to survive as long as there was water somewhere on the planet.

Throughout the last four billion years, Earth has remained a place where life could exist. Its temperature never got so cold that all the liquid water froze, and its atmosphere did not slowly drift away into space or freeze out onto the surface.

Mars is a different story. It did not have quite as tight a grip on its atmosphere, it did not have as much internal heat, and it received less warmth from the sun. As time went on, Mars' once-thick atmosphere became thin, and its temperature dropped. Water, the key to life, vanished from its surface. If life did begin on Mars, it could have survived only in watery underground oases.

EXTREMOPHILES

Life on Earth is much more hardy, diverse, and adaptable than scientists used to think. Bacteria live in some of the harshest environments on Earth—places that were once thought to be lifeless. These bacteria are called extremophiles (which means "lovers of extremes") because they have adapted to live in places that are very hot, or very cold, or very extreme in some other way.

Some bacteria live in the boiling-hot waters near deep-sea volcanic vents. Superheated, mineral-rich water billows out of these undersea chimneys from deep inside the Earth. Heat-loving bacteria grow on their outside walls. These bacteria stop growing if the temperature drops below 200 degrees Fahrenheit—the water's too cold for them!

Other types of bacteria flourish in the coldest places on Earth. Vast parts of the Arctic and Antarctic are frozen solid most of the year, but cold-loving bacteria make their home in these icy wastes, floating on chunks of frozen ocean water.

The strangest extremophiles may be the ones that dwell deep underground, inside almost-solid rock. Trickles of water seep into the rock and keep them alive, but their home is scorching hot and there is no space to grow. Some of these strange bacteria may live for thousands of years.

Before scientists discovered extremophiles, they never imagined that life could exist in such alien environments. Now it appears that on Earth, wherever there is even a small amount of water, there is life.

Deep-sea volcanic vents, such as this one more than 10,000 feet below the surface of the Atlantic Ocean, are home to heat-loving bacteria and other "extreme" life forms.

For over three billion years, microscopic organisms were the only inhabitants of Earth. And for most of this time, these tiny living things were extremely primitive. But slowly, things began to change.

Some of these microorganisms evolved clever new ways to get nourishment from their environment. Eventually, the descendants of the first primitive cells evolved the ability to use the energy in sunlight and the carbon dioxide in air to make food. This process is called photosynthesis. As part of photosynthesis, oxygen is released into the atmosphere.

By one billion years ago, vast chains of photosynthesizing bacteria formed slimy mats on the banks of streams. Green algae floated near the ocean surface and clung to rocky shores at low tide. Steadily, oxygen bubbled out of the waters and drifted up into the air.

Eventually, about half a billion years ago, simple green plants began to spread across the land. At first, they were very small and could grow only where it was very wet. Later, plants of all sizes and shapes, some with colorful flowers and fruit, grew farther and farther from the water's edge. But life depends on water. So these plants evolved roots that could drink from underground, instead of having to rely on the morning dew or an afternoon rain.

Once green plants began to cover the land, other forms of life were able to follow. Plants provided food and shelter for other living things. By about 100 million years ago, grasshoppers chewed on young leaves, mushrooms digested fallen logs, frogs hid in the marsh grasses, and birds nested in the branches of bushes. Human beings have inhabited Earth for only a few hundred thousand years—just the last instant of our planet's long history.

Earth today is far different from the barren planet it used to be. Even a handful of soil from a forest is packed with microbes and insects. Even a cup of water from a stream is brimming with bacteria and algae.

→ Earth

↓ Mars

for centuries. Geologists have collected samples of rock and soil from Antarctica to Tibet. Chemists have analyzed samples of air from around the globe, and biologists have examined ancient fossils from every continent.

It is much harder to study the rocks, soil, and air of a planet that is millions of miles away. No geologists, biologists, or chemists have ever explored Mars. Only robot spacecraft have visited its surface, and all of them are still parked there on the dusty Martian plains. None has brought bags of Martian rocks back to Earth.

Scientists have only the smallest trickle of data from Mars. But that is changing. The launches of *Mars Pathfinder* and *Mars Global Surveyor* began a decade-long robotic assault on the Red Planet. They were followed by the *Mars Polar Lander*. And many more spacecraft will follow these. Now, every 26 months, when Earth and Mars are favorably aligned in their orbits, new spacecraft will rocket toward the Red Planet. This fleet of spacecraft— orbiters, landers, and rovers—will study the planet, search for clues to the disappearance of its water, and eventually bring precious Martian rocks back to scientists on Earth.

Launch of the Mars Polar Lander *from Cape Canaveral, Florida, in January 1999.*

What happened to all the water on Mars? The *Polar Lander* will investigate that question when it settles down near the frosty fringe of Mars' south polar icecap. It will gather data during the late Martian spring and early summer, a time of year when the sun never sets on this part of the planet. Scientists hope that the layers of ice and dust at the edge of the icecap will reveal how Mars' climate has changed over the past several thousands to millions of years. This will give them clues to the fate of the water that once flowed on the planet.

The *Polar Lander* carries a microphone that will be the first to record the sounds of Mars. Maybe it will hear howling winds or crackling thunder. Maybe it will hear only the scraping sounds of its own robot arm scooping up samples of soil.

The mission will also peer underground. Two microprobes will slam into the planet's surface at over 400 miles per hour and tunnel about four feet into the icy Martian ground. They will look for water ice below the surface and radio their findings to the orbiting spacecraft, which will relay them to Earth.

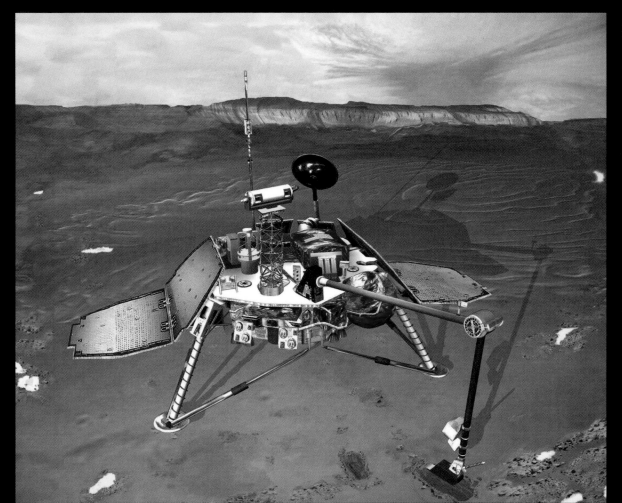

← *Artist's rendering of the* Mars Polar Lander.

↓ *Part of the landing site selected for the* Mars Polar Lander. (Mars Global Surveyor)

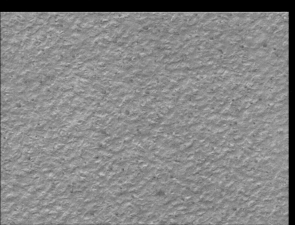

A little more than two years later, *Mars Surveyor 2001* will enter orbit around the planet. This orbiter will carry instruments to detect and map the minerals on Mars. The instruments will be sensitive enough to search for sites where water collected in pools. When the water disappeared, minerals would have been left behind on the surface. Instruments will also search for places where ancient hot springs bubbled. The hot, mineral-rich water would have cooled quickly when it reached the surface. As it cooled, minerals would have been deposited on the ground, and any microbes in the water would have been trapped. If the orbiting spacecraft finds deposits of those minerals, future landers will almost certainly be sent down for a closer look. These would be perfect places to search for microscopic fossils.

Surveyor will also look for volcanic vents and hot springs by searching for small warm spots on the otherwise frigid planet. These would be fantastic discoveries, because they would be places to search for microscopic living things.

While *Surveyor* is orbiting Mars, yet another lander will visit the surface. It will land near the equator, in the ancient highlands, probably close to an old crater. A small rover, named *Marie Curie* after the Nobel Prize–winning physicist, will roam around near the landing site. *Marie Curie*, almost identical to *Sojourner*, will search for rocks that might tell the tale of conditions on ancient Mars.

METEORITES FROM MARS

Even though no spacecraft has brought Martian rocks back to Earth, 12 small pieces of Mars have made the long trip on their own. Their separate journeys had violent beginnings and lasted millions of years. Each was blasted into space by a huge meteor impact. Each eventually wandered too near Earth and was captured by its gravity. Some of these meteorites from Mars crashed into Antarctica thousands of years ago and have only recently been found. Others were seen streaking through the skies over India and France in the 1800s. Astonished townspeople followed their fiery trails and found the potato-sized rocks shortly after they hit the ground.

How do scientists know that these meteorites came from Mars? All 12 have about the same composition, so they came from the same place in the solar system. Most of the 12 are young rocks, so they came from a volcanically active planet, not an ancient asteroid. The best evidence comes from small bubbles of gas trapped inside some of these rocks. The composition of this gas is the same as that of the air the Viking *landers sampled on Mars.*

These messengers from Mars hold valuable clues to the planet's past. Scientists discovered carbonates inside one of them. This may be more evidence that there was once water on Mars. It is also possible that, if there was ever life on Mars, evidence of it might be locked inside some of the meteorites. Scientists are examining bits of them under powerful microscopes, looking for microfossils or other signs that living things once inhabited the rocks. They have found some intriguing things, but so far no proof of ancient life.

Until spacecraft return to Earth with fresh samples of Martian rocks, these meteorites are the only pieces of Mars that scientists have to study.

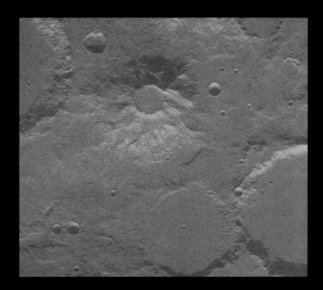

↑ *Ancient volcanoes, like this one in the southern highlands, may once have had volcanic vents and hot springs.* (Viking)

← *Artist's rendering of the* Mars Surveyor 2001 *orbiter, lander, and rover* Marie Curie.

In 2003, Earth and Mars will again be in the right positions for engineers to launch a group of spacecraft. One might carry a small airplane designed to catch the Martian winds and soar miles through the Martian skies. Another will carry a lander and a rover that will search for evidence of ancient surface water. This lander might settle down near a large crater where the rocks from deep underground were blasted to the surface by a meteor impact. These rocks may have been formed in the presence of water long ago. The rover will collect samples of rocks and soil and then put them in the nose of a small rocket. The rocket will launch the container into orbit around Mars in hopes that a later spacecraft will carry it back to Earth.

Those hopes may be realized in 2008. That is when a retriever spacecraft is scheduled to return from the first round trip to Mars. The mission will last more than two years, but the spacecraft will finally ferry about one pound of Martian rocks to eager scientists back on Earth.

These priceless pieces of Mars will be whisked to a quarantine facility to be sure that they do not carry alien microbes that might be harmful to living things on Earth. Then scientists will use sophisticated laboratory equipment to study the samples. They will look for clues to conditions on early Mars and even for traces of ancient microbes.

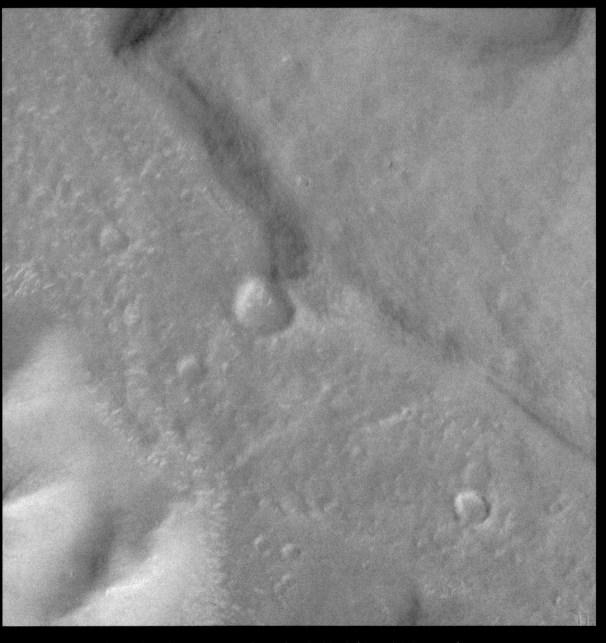

Water may once have flowed through Gusev Crater in the southern highlands. (Mars Global Surveyor)

One day astronauts will make the long journey to Mars. When they step out of their spacecraft onto the red Martian soil, they will become the first human beings to visit another planet. This expedition will extend our presence farther into the solar system. It will be the adventure of a lifetime.

Astronauts will explore Mars the way scientists explore remote areas of Earth. Over many missions, they will plunge shovels into dry riverbeds and chip rocks from steep canyon walls. They will drive buggies over windswept dunes and hike across lava fields and up the slopes of extinct volcanoes. They will drill deep into the frozen ground for traces of subsurface water. If robot scouts have located ancient hot springs, astronauts will scour these sites for rocks and minerals that may contain microscopic evidence of life.

Earth and Mars share a common beginning. But the two planets evolved very differently. Why did Mars follow one path while Earth followed another? As we investigate the mysteries of Mars, we are also learning things that help us understand our own planet and how it came to be the oasis that we know today.

Mars Mission Time Line

1964–1965 *Mariner 4*

Flew past Mars in July 1965 at a distance of 6,000 miles, sending back 22 photographs, which showed craters on Mars' surface for the first time.

1969 *Mariner 6 and Mariner 7*

Both flew within 2,200 miles of Mars, sending back more than 200 photographs.

1971 *Mariner 9*

Orbited Mars, becoming the first spacecraft to orbit a planet other than Earth. Sent back more than 7,000 TV pictures, showing such features as Olympus Mons, Valles Marineris, and Mars' moons, Phobos and Deimos.

1971 *Mars 3*

A probe containing science experiments launched by the Soviet Union. Landed on the surface of Mars but fell silent after 20 seconds of operation. Several similar missions to Mars launched by the Soviet Union in 1971 and 1973 were also unsuccessful.

1975–1976 *Viking 1 and Viking 2*

On July 20, 1976, *Viking 1* became the first spacecraft to land successfully on Mars, followed several weeks later by *Viking 2*. Both landers returned photographs and other data and conducted experiments to search for primitive life. Meanwhile, the *Viking 1* and *Viking 2* orbiters photographed the Martian surface.

1996–1997 *Pathfinder*

Landed on Mars on July 4, 1997. *Pathfinder* sent back thousands of photographs of the surface, and its six-wheeled rover *Sojourner* became the first vehicle to explore another planet.

1996–2001 *Mars Global Surveyor*

Orbiting spacecraft designed to survey Mars for a full Martian year. Instruments include cameras and the Mars Orbiter Laser Altimeter, which measures the height of features on the surface.

— *Image of Phobos.* (Mars Global Surveyor)

— Viking *lander.*

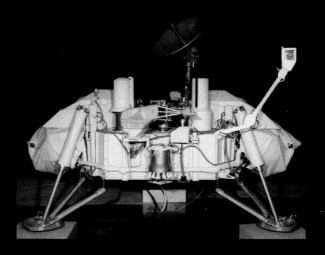

46

	Mars	Earth
Distance from sun:	128–155 million miles	91–94 million miles
Diameter:	4,219 miles	7,926 miles
Length of year:	687 days	365 days
Length of day:	24 hours 37 minutes	24 hours
Moons:	Two: Phobos and Deimos	One

1998–1999 *Mars Climate Orbiter*

Entered orbit around Mars in September 1999 to study the planet's atmosphere, climate, and surface.

1999 *Mars Polar Lander*

Launched in January 1999 and scheduled to land near Mars' south pole in December 1999. Equipped with cameras, experiments to study soil, a microphone, and two micro-probes that will penetrate the Martian surface to look for water ice.

2001 *Mars Surveyor 2001*

Will include an orbiter, a lander, and a rover similar to *Sojourner.* Instruments include a camera that will record the spacecraft's descent and landing on the Martian surface.

Mars Polar Lander *being prepared for launch in 1998.*

Web resources:

www.nasa.gov
NASA's home page, with current space news and links to other NASA sites.

www.nasa.gov/kids.html
Dozens of links to NASA sites designed for young people.

mars.jpl.nasa.gov
Home page for NASA and the Jet Propulsion Laboratory's Mars missions, with links to other Mars mission web sites.

mars.jpl.nasa.gov/mgs
Mars Global Surveyor home page, with up-to-date news, photographs, and real-time animation of the spacecraft.

mars.jpl.nasa.gov/MPF
Pathfinder mission home page, including photo archives.

mars.jpl.nasa.gov/msp98
Home page for *Mars Climate Orbiter* and *Mars Polar Lander.*

mars.jpl.nasa.gov/2001
News and plans for the *Mars Surveyor 2001* mission.

nssdc.gsfc.nasa.gov/planetary/mars
National Science Data Center's Mars web site. Includes pages on the history of Mars exploration a virtual "tour" of Mars, and links to other Mars science sites.

photojournal.jpl.nasa.gov
NASA's online photo archive, with hundreds of downloadable pictures of the planets.

47

Index

Picture credits: **Air Force Chart and Information Center:** 8 *bottom right.* **Lowell Observatory:** 8 *left & top right.* **Magrath Photography/Photo Researchers, Inc:** 3. **Malin Space Science Systems and JPL/NASA:** 13 *right,* 15, 17 *right,* 23 *right,* 26 *left & right,* 28 *left, center, & bottom right,* 41 *right,* 43. **Geoffrey McCormack:** 6, 7, 13 *top right,* 29, 31. **B. Murton/Photo Researchers, Inc:** 38. **NASA:** 4 *left,* 10 *left,* 14, 16 *bottom,* 22, 25, 26 *center,* 37 *top.* **NASA/JPL/Caltech:** 4 *right,* 9 *left,* 11, 13 *bottom left,* 18, 19, 20, 21, 23 *left,* 24, 27, 28 *top right,* 37, 39 *left,* 40, 41 *left,* 42, 44, 46, 47. **NASA/MOLA Science Team:** 17 *left.* **NASA/NSSDC:** 9 *right.* **NASA/USGS:** 5, 10 *right,* 12, 16 *top,* 36. **Pat Rawlings:** 45. **Michael Rothman:** 30, 33, 35. **United States Geological Survey:** 13 *top left.* **F. Stuart Westmorland:** 39 *right.*